Learning About Unicorns

by Laura Alden
illustrated by Krystyna Stasiak

 CHILDRENS PRESS, CHICAGO

Dedication:
   To Lorraine Mulligan Davis

Library of Congress Cataloging in Publication Data

Alden, Laura, 1955-
   Learning about unicorns.

   (The Learning about series)
   Summary: A collection of legends, folktales, and
lore revealing the origins, history, habits, and
powers of unicorns.
   1. Unicorns—Juvenile literature.   [1. Unicorns.
2. Folklore]   I. Stasiak, Krystyna, ill.   II. Title.
III. Series.
GR830.U6A43   1985   398.2'454   85-9926
ISBN 0-516-06539-4

Learning About Unicorns

created by THE CHILD'S WORLD

There's a rustling in the bushes, an outline in the trees. There's a flash in the dark. Something is there. Something strange. Something mysterious.

Stop. Look. Maybe you won't see anything. But maybe if you wait, you will. You may glimpse the shape of a horse with a horn. It might be a unicorn—a unicorn who is watching you.

Unicorns, though, are usually hard to see. They live around the edges of our minds. We see them out of the corners of our eyes. Yet when we turn to look, there is nothing there. Unicorns are magical (and very, very quick).

Those who know say unicorns are most often seen near water. Waterfalls are best. That's because a unicorn likes to drink with its head up, so it can watch for hunters. Some would kill the creature for its horn. The horn of a unicorn can heal any sickness. It can make any water pure. Or so they say.

But the best way to find a unicorn is to find one asleep. On matted ferns or on soft green moss, the unicorn sleeps and dreams. And if you sit by it quietly, you will dream too. You will dream dreams of long ago kingdoms and times now forgotten. You will dream of what was—and of what might have been.

Unicorns have lived in many lands. They come in different shapes and sizes. Some are hunters. Some are fighters. All have a magical horn. But where did all these unicorns come from? Who saw the first unicorn? Who sees them still?

THE FIRST UNICORNS

There are many legends of unicorns, from every time and place. A legend is made up of many stories. Part of a legend may be true. From the middle east comes the legend of

THE FIRST ANIMAL NAMED.*

When the world was made, so were its creatures. There were many kinds of creatures. But only two of them had names—Adam and Eve. It was Adam's job to name the animals. So he called them together. A glint caught his eye. It was a horn, a single horn. "You are Unicorn!" Adam cried.

Unicorn became Adam and Eve's friend and guide. They rode on its back to get around (and just for fun). Unicorn loved Adam and Eve. And they were very happy in the garden where they lived.

Then one sad day, Unicorn saw Adam and Eve driven from the garden. Flaming swords burned at the entrance! Unicorn cried out to its friends. But Adam and Eve could never return. Unicorn

*A legend—not the creation story of the Bible.

took one last look at the garden. Then it leaped through the fiery gate. Unicorn knew there was no way back. But, out of love, it gave up the garden for its friends.

In the far east, people said the unicorn helped to make the world. Then, they said it fled into the forest and was hardly ever seen. But one day a Chinese emperor saw one. And he received

THE GIFT OF THE UNICORN.

Fu Hsi sat beside the Yellow River. The water moved slowly by and was gone. It was like life, thought Fu Hsi. People move through life without leaving anything behind.

Then across the river, Fu Hsi saw a unicorn. It looked like a calf, but had the scales of a dragon. From its head grew a silver horn. The unicorn waded through the river. Wherever it stepped, the muddy water became clear! And the unicorn dropped a trail of emeralds behind him.

The creature drew near. Fu Hsi saw that its back was covered with magic signs and symbols. Fu Hsi stared at the lines and squiggles on the beast's back. He grabbed a stick and traced the symbols in the dirt.

From these lines came the Chinese alphabet. After that, thoughts of people could live after them. For words could be written and remembered. And so can stories about unicorns.

Some people think unicorns only lived long ago. Unicorns are no more, they think. The last unicorn, says one poem, was

THE LATE PASSENGER.*

Noah's son, Ham, looked around in a pout. The ark was a mess. And he had just cleaned it that morning. I'll be scrubbing the rest of my life, thought Ham. Then Ham had an idea. He would shut the ark door—just for the night. No more animals; no more scrubbing until morning! Slam! Ham pulled the door closed. Noah didn't know. He was counting noses (and toes). But soon there came a knock on the ark door and the sound of crying.

"Who is knocking?" Noah called to Ham. "What's going on? Open up, open up! Take all animals in. Even a duck won't live through this."

Ham tried not to hear. It started to rain. The crying went on, forever, say some. For Ham had locked out the unicorn. And Noah and Ham never saw one again.

Never leave a unicorn out in the rain.

*A fictional story—not the Biblical account of Noah.

EVERYWHERE A UNICORN

The unicorn legends grew and grew. And they spread from East to West.

During the Middle Ages, people in Europe enjoyed hearing stories about unicorns. So much so, that they even made up new stories about the creatures.

The unicorn became a symbol for new beginnings. It was a favorite of young girls. (That was because people said unicorns laid their heads in the laps of true maidens.)

The unicorn was a symbol for many things during past centuries. For a while, it was even used as a symbol for Christ.

Those were great days for unicorn stories.

Often, in the Middle Ages, a unicorn would show up with famous people. Some even say a unicorn changed history, as in the story of

THE UNICORN AND GENGHIS KHAN.

Genghis Khan was a fighter from Mongolia. And he was a winner too. His empire stretched from Korea to Persia. But Khan wanted more. So in 1224, Khan's army marched toward India. And no one could stop him. No one dared. Khan climbed the mountains until he reached the last one. He was ready to conquer India.

But no one was there to fight! No soldiers at least. There was only a small green beast with a red and black horn. A unicorn, thought Khan. What could this mean?

The unicorn spoke four languages. But it did not say much. Instead, the small green animal knelt three times at Khan's feet. A feeling crept over Khan. He only had that feeling when his father was around. Then Genghis Khan was afraid. For his father had died years before.

Khan did not move. Khan's army grew restless. For the first time in his life, Genghis Khan feared.

At last Khan called to his men. "Turn back," he said. "My father has warned me not to go on." Khan looked at his small friend. The unicorn lifted its head and was gone.

So it was that Genghis Khan marched back down the mountain. And India was saved.

A little unicorn goes a long way.

The most famous unicorn story of all was told 500 years ago. It was told in seven pictures called tapestries. The tapestries were made, thread by thread, by weavers in Brussels. They told of

THE HUNT OF THE UNICORN.

The nobles met at dawn in their tunics and tights. They planned to hunt the unicorn. Others came to protest their plans. "Do not hunt the unicorn," they begged the lord. But the lord only laughed and called for his dogs. "Ho!" he waved. "Ha!" They were off with their horns and their hounds.

The woods were damp. The hounds sniffed the ground. Then there it was! The dogs barked and danced. The air filled with spice—unicorn scent! The unicorn stood by a stream. Its hooves were silver; its eyes a bright blue. Its pearly horn was well-ridged and well-worn. Animals stood beside it. It knelt at the stream. Then, slowly, it dipped in the tip of its horn. The stream gurgled and was clean. But when the other animals jumped in to bathe and to drink, the unicorn ran.

The hunters ran after the unicorn. The unicorn ran through the woods by the stream. The hunters far outnumbered the creature. When it again leaped into the stream, they surrounded it. A spear pierced the unicorn's side.

Escape! Sad and wounded, the unicorn ran to find a place to rest. Then, near the castle, it saw three women sitting. (Now unicorns like young women. Young women seem gentle and kind. And they do not usually hunt unicorns!) The unicorn liked one woman best. But she was crying. The unicorn laid its head in her lap to comfort her. And then the dogs were upon it. The hunters were too. The woman tricked the unicorn! Tricked and trapped, the unicorn was killed. The young woman vanished. The town got ready to celebrate.

But there is one more tapestry. And in it, the unicorn though chained, lives again. Just like magic.

(You can see the seven unicorn tapestries at The Cloisters, a part of the Metropolitan Museum of Art in New York City.)

In the following story from Italy, the unicorn brings sadness to

THE WOOD NYMPH.

Once a man saw a wood nymph on his way home from hunting. The nymph was dressed in the color of mist. A bow and arrows hung from her waist. The man fell in love with her that minute. But when the nymph saw the man, she ran into the woods. The man chased her. Now nymphs know their woods, so the man did not catch her. Still, he did not give up, but lived in the woods to be near her. And he carved a reed flute and played it each night. Nymphs love music. That much he knew.

At last the nymph came. She danced for the man. And each night after that, she danced and he played. But the nymph would not go back with the man to his land.

Then one night, the nymph did not come. The man waited and played and finally slept. He dreamed that a figure came and stood over him. The figure spoke in a terrible voice. ''It is forbidden,'' it said. ''A mortal shall not love a wood nymph.''

The man awoke. He felt himself change. His neck grew longer. His arms became legs. And then, a horn pushed out from his forehead! The man jumped and ran, no, galloped about. The nymph! He must find her. Would she love him still?

He found her at last. But she turned and took aim. ''My love!'' he cried. But his voice was strange. And she did not know him. The arrow pierced his heart. Tears mixed with his blood. And the nymph wept, too, for her lost love.

But most stories about the unicorn tell of its powers. In Russia, this story is told of

THE MAGICAL HORN.

It was a long, hot summer in the Crimea. Hotter than usual. Water was scarce. In one village, people had only enough water to drink. There was no washing allowed. So dust and dirt covered the town. Then typhoid struck. At first, sick people thought they were just thirsty and dirty. Then one woman saw rosy spots on her husband's chest. Another saw them on her daughter. The women burned fires around their houses. They hung herbs in the doorways. But the spots spread through the town.

Then someone thought of a unicorn's horn. The horn could heal anyone. Some scoffed. But some did not. They planned how to catch a unicorn. To do so, they needed a young woman with no husband or children. But there was not such a woman in their town!

"Then I'll catch a unicorn," said a woman named Katya.

"But you have children," another said.

"Unicorns trust those who would help others." said Katya. "I know I am not perfect. Still, I would like to try."

So the women walked behind Katya in a line to the lake. They waited while Katya sat, her hands in her lap. At last, a unicorn came, late in the day. It drew near. Then it stopped. With its eyes on Katya, the beast stepped back. Katya met its gaze. A minute

went by. Then the unicorn stepped gently forward. It laid its head right in Katya's lap.

Katya led the unicorn back into town. At each well the creature dipped its horn. The water bubbled and became pure! Then Katya took the unicorn to each house. The creature held its horn over those who were ill. They felt better at once.

At dawn, Katya led the healer back out of town. A crowd came along. One man whispered, "What if the sickness comes back?" Another man said, "The magic is in the horn. We must have the horn."

So the men killed the unicorn and kept its horn. Katya, in horror, moved far away. And when sickness came again to that town, no unicorn came.

You don't get a second chance with a unicorn.

Not-so-nice unicorns get caught, too. That's what happens in
the story of

THE BRAVE LITTLE TAILOR.

One day while sewing, a tailor killed seven flies at once. Now
the flies had been quite a bother. So the tailor wanted to tell the
world. ''Seven at one blow!'' he stitched on his belt. ''The whole
world shall hear it!''

SEVEN AT ONE BLOW

The tailor set out to tell the world. By and by, he came to a king's castle. The king's men read the tailor's belt. They told the king of the tailor's claim. So the king hired the tailor into his service. But the soldiers did not like the tailor. They went to the king to quit. "You have one who can kill seven at one blow," they said. "What do you need us for?"

This made the king sad. He liked the tailor. But he knew that the tailor must go. "Capture the unicorn who roams the woods," he told the tailor. "If you do, you can marry my daughter and have half of my kingdom." The king, of course, knew the unicorn to be mean.

The tailor thought this was a good offer. So he went to find the unicorn. He did not have long to wait. The unicorn found him. The beast charged. Its head was down, and its horn aimed at the tailor's heart. The tailor stood still. Then—quick!—the brave little tailor jumped behind a tree.

THUNK! The unicorn's horn stuck in the tree! The tailor bridled the beast. He chopped the tree to free its horn. Then he went back to the king, leading the unicorn.

The king wasn't pleased. He gave the tailor more tasks. But at last, the king kept his promises. And neither flies nor unicorns ever bothered the tailor again.

*To obtain this folk tale in its entirety, see
    page 47.

STILL LOOKING FOR UNICORNS

Few unicorns are reported today. Instead, unicorns star in cartoons. They come as stuffed toys. They get carved into rocking horses. They are pictured on posters. But there is still something nice about unicorns. We really are still looking for them. In fact, the Barnum and Bailey Circus, in early 1985, claimed to have four of the one-horned beasts. And the circus featured them in many of their shows. Television news reports included them, and photographs of the animals were printed in the newspapers across the country. But, the circus's claim to having real unicorns was protested. And we were told that the animals were goats, not unicorns. However, the circus's claim tells us that interest in unicorns continues.

And so the legends grow. Stories from past centuries are retold. New stories are written. Here are a few stories written in this century that are contributing to the growth of the legends.

Most unicorns do not have wings. (Their magic makes them *seem* to fly when they leap and run.) But there is at least one winged unicorn. Madeleine L'Engle wrote about him in *A Swiftly Tilting Planet.* His name was

GAUDIOR.

"I will blow up the world!" cried Mad Dog Branzillo. And everyone knew he would. But Charles Wallace Murry was given one last chance to save the world. And from a star came a unicorn to help him. Gaudior was a flying unicorn. He flew not just through space, but through time. (In fact, he said time-flying was more fun.)

The two traveled into the past world to save the present one. Evil forces tried to stop them. But Gaudior had power, too. And he had to use it all to keep Charles Wallace alive.

As they traveled together, Charles Wallace learned a lot about flying unicorns. They sing in the sky. They eat only starlight and moonlight. And their young hatch from eggs.

But Charles Wallace learned much more than that. He learned that one person can make a difference in the world.

And so can one unicorn.

Unicorns usually work alone. They rarely get together. But Joan Aiken tells of unicorns that appeared in a group on

UNICORN TUESDAY.

Monday was the day for strange things to happen at the Armitage's. (For that was the day the Armitage children—Mark and Harriet—were usually home with the sitter.) But it was Tuesday. So no one was expecting a strange happening. But Mark reported one—he said there was a unicorn in the garden.

After breakfast, Harriet rushed to the garden. And there, among the flowers, stood a unicorn.

The creature was lovely—"snow-white all over, with shining green eyes and a twisted mother-of-pearl horn in the middle of its forehead."

When Mr. Armitage walked out into the garden and spotted the unicorn, he exclaimed, "But today is *Tuesday*."

Before long, their doorbell rang, and a policeman stood at the door.

"Is it true that you are keeping a unicorn without a license?" asked the policeman.

"It just arrived. I don't know if we're going to keep it or not," replied Mr. Armitage.

"Oh, please let's buy the license and keep the unicorn," Harriet urged.

"That will be 10,000 gold pieces," said the officer.

The unicorn came up with the gold. Each burr Mark combed from the unicorn's tail turned to gold. (And the unicorn had lots of burrs!) But then, stranger things started to happen. And the strangest of all was that 100 more unicorns showed up in the garden!

The Armitages put up a sign. UNICORNS GIVEN AWAY. QUIET TO RIDE OR DRIVE. The people in the town were shocked. They thought it was a bad joke. But the unicorns were given away free. So it was a good joke.

In the end, all the unicorns got good homes. And the Armitages kept their unicorn too.

Even though it *was* Tuesday.

*To find out where you can obtain more of the story,
   see page 47.

UNICORNS GIVEN AWAY
QUIET TO RIDE OR DRIVE

Most people today have never seen a unicorn. Some say there are none left. Peter S. Beagle wrote about a creature who thought she was

THE LAST UNICORN.

"The unicorn lived in a lilac wood, and she lived all alone." That's how the story begins. One day the unicorn heard that no one saw unicorns anymore. Come to think of it, she hadn't seen any others lately either.

She wondered if she really was alone. Were all the others really gone? She tried not to let it bother her. But she had no peace. She couldn't be happy not knowing if she was alone in the world.

Finally, she woke up in the middle of one warm night. She knew she must find out.

So the unicorn left the woods to look for her kind. Time quickly passed. Summer turned to winter and back again.

The road was long and hard. But she continued.

Along the way, a magician named Schmendrick joined her. So did Molly Grue. They travelled through forests and towns, always hoping to catch a glimpse of a unicorn. Or hear from the townspeople that their woods was the home of other unicorns.

But none of the people had seen unicorns for a long time. In fact, it had been so long that they would not know a unicorn if they saw one. They thought the unicorn was a white horse. (That is very insulting to a unicorn.)

Still the unicorn went on. She had to find out where all the other unicorns had gone. She heard about a curse. She heard about a mean king and big, bad, red bull. That's enough to make anyone turn back! But Schmendrick, Molly, and the unicorn did not turn back.

They finally found the unicorns. But not until Schmendrick made the unicorn human and then unicorn again. Not until a skull talked and a castle crumbled. And not until the unicorn faced the red bull. Then they knew where the unicorns had gone—and why.

The last unicorn wasn't really last. And maybe she still isn't.

So if you haven't seen a unicorn lately, don't give up. When your friends laugh at you, only smile. And when they ask, "Seen any unicorns?" just say, "Not yet."

Then keep an eye on the trees.

Index

For More Information

''The Late Passenger'' story is based on a poem by C.S. Lewis
from Narrative Poems, edited by Walter Hooper

''The Brave Little Tailor'' can be found in its entirety in
A Book of Giants by Ruth Manning-Sanders.

The Joan Aiken story is entitled, ''Yes, But Today Is Tuesday''
and appears in Legendary Animals, edited by Bryna and
Louis Untermeyer.